THE BEAUTY
OF THE HUSBAND

THE BEAUTY
OF THE HUSBAND

a fictional essay

in

29

tangos

Anne Carson

Alfred A. Knopf

New York

2001

THIS IS A BORZOI BOOK
PUBLISHED BY ALFRED A. KNOPF

www.aaknopf.com

Knopf, Borzoi Books and the colophon are registered
trademarks of Random House, Inc.

Portions of this work (tangos IX, XIV, XXIII and XXV) were
previously published in *The London Review of Books*.

Library of Congress Cataloging-in-Publication Data
Carson, Anne, [date]
The beauty of the husband : a fictional essay in 29 tangos /
by Anne Carson. — 1st. ed.
p.   cm.
ISBN 0-375-40804-5 (alk. paper)
1. Married people—Poetry.   2. Marriage—Poetry.   3. Adultery—Poetry.   I. Title.
PS3553.A7667 B43 2001
811'.54—dc21   00-062002

Manufactured in the United States of America
First Edition

THE BEAUTY
OF THE HUSBAND

                                              more
Bad reasons for her sorrow, as appears
In the famed memoirs of a thousand years
Written by Crafticant

JOHN KEATS,
The Jealousies: A Faery Tale,
by Lucy Vaughan Lloyd of China Walk,
Lambeth, lines 84–87

I. I DEDICATE THIS BOOK TO KEATS (IS IT YOU WHO TOLD ME KEATS WAS A DOCTOR?) ON GROUNDS THAT A DEDICATION HAS TO BE FLAWED IF A BOOK IS TO REMAIN FREE AND FOR HIS GENERAL SURRENDER TO BEAUTY

A wound gives off its own light

surgeons say.

If all the lamps in the house were turned out

you could dress this wound

by what shines from it.

Fair reader I offer merely an analogy.

A delay.

"Use delay instead of picture or painting—

a delay in glass

as you would say a poem in prose or a spittoon in silver."

So Duchamp

of *The Bride Stripped Bare by Her Bachelors*

which broke in eight pieces in transit from the Brooklyn Museum

to Connecticut (1912).

What is being delayed?

Marriage I guess.

That swaying place as my husband called it.

Look how the word

shines.

Tis chosen I hear from Hymen's jewelry,
And you will prize it, lady, I doubt not,
Beyond all pleasures past and all to come.

JOHN KEATS,
Otho the Great: A Tragedy in Five Acts, 1.1.137–39

II. BUT A DEDICATION IS ONLY FELICITOUS IF PERFORMED BEFORE WITNESSES—IT IS AN ESSENTIALLY PUBLIC SURRENDER LIKE THAT OF STANDARDS OF BATTLE

You know I was married years ago and when he left my husband took my notebooks.

Wirebound notebooks.

You know that cool sly verb *write*. He liked writing, disliked having to start

each thought himself.

Used my starts to various ends, for example in a pocket I found a letter he'd begun

(to his mistress at that time)

containing a phrase I had copied from Homer: ἐντροπαλιζομένη is how Homer says

Andromache went

after she parted from Hektor—"often turning to look back"

she went

down from Troy's tower and through stone streets to her loyal husband's

house and there

with her women raised a lament for a living man in his own halls.

Loyal to nothing

my husband. So why did I love him from early girlhood to late middle age

and the divorce decree came in the mail?

Beauty. No great secret. Not ashamed to say I loved him for his beauty.

As I would again

if he came near. Beauty convinces. You know beauty makes sex possible.

Beauty makes sex sex.

You if anyone grasp this—hush, let's pass

to natural situations.

Other species, which are not poisonous, often have colorations and patterns

similar to poisonous species.

This imitation of a poisonous by a nonpoisonous species is called *mimicry*.

My husband was no mimic.

You will mention of course the war games. I complained to you often enough
when they were here all night
with the boards spread out and rugs and little lamps and cigarettes like Napoleon's
tent I suppose,
who could sleep? All in all my husband was a man who knew more
about the Battle of Borodino
than he did about his own wife's body, much more! Tensions poured up the walls
and along the ceiling,
sometimes they played Friday night till Monday morning straight through, he
and his pale wrathful friends.
They sweated badly. They ate meats of the countries in play.
Jealousy
formed no small part of my relationship to the Battle of Borodino.

I hate it.
Do you.
Why play all night.
The time is real.
It's a game.
It's a real game.
Is that a quote.
Come here.
No.
I need to touch you.
No.
Yes.

That night we made love "the real way" which we had not yet attempted
although married six months.

Big mystery. No one knew where to put their leg and to this day I'm not sure we got it right.

He seemed happy. You're like Venice he said beautifully.

Early next day

I wrote a short talk ("On Defloration") which he stole and had published in a small quarterly magazine.

Overall this was a characteristic interaction between us.

Or should I say ideal.

Neither of us had ever seen Venice.

Will you return, Prince, to our banquetting?

JOHN KEATS,
Otho the Great: A Tragedy in Five Acts, 1.2.152

III. AND FINALLY A GOOD DEDICATION IS INDIRECT (OVERHEARD, ETC.) AS IF VERDI'S "LA DONNA È MOBILE" HAD BEEN A POEM SCRATCHED ON GLASS

His mistress at that time—indeed the very concept "mistress" for him—was French.
Friends of his told me that she didn't wash and in bars was inclined
to order liters of champagne on his tab.

I can imagine how he would frown, curse, sigh, lift his hands and adore it.
He took me to a movie about a bookshop in Paris
whose owner liked to have his assistant

mount a ladder to fetch a book then he slides his hand up her leg.
Just that—one hand, momentary. Her blush heats the theater.
Every time he said Go, up she went.

How do people get power over one another he said wonderingly as we came out
onto the street. Bruises too filled him with curiosity.
I could not meet this need,

I hear she did. The reason I mention washing is that it puzzled me why
none of this seemed unclean in his study of it.
None of it was orgasmic for him,

his thrust—analytic you could say, as if discovering a new crystal.
Is innocence just one of the disguises of beauty?
He could fill structures of

threat with a light like the earliest olive oil. I began to understand *nature*
as something seamed and deep into which one plunged, going dark.
Yes I am delaying again.

Clothed in flames and rolling through the sky is how I felt the night he told me
he had a mistress and with shy pride
slid out a photograph.

I can't see the face I said angrily, throwing it down. He looked at me.
We were at a window (restaurant) high above the street,
married a little more than a year.

Quick work I said. Are you going to be arch he said.
I broke the glass and jumped.
Now of course you know

that isn't the true story, what broke wasn't glass, what fell to earth wasn't body.
But still when I recall the conversation it's what I see—me a fighter pilot
bailing out over the channel. Me as kill.

Oh no we're not enemies he said. I love you! I love you both.
Is it not Mr. Rochester who grinds his teeth and tells us
in less than two minutes with its gliding green hiss

jealousy can eat to a heart's core, this formula having occurred to him
as he sat in the musk and amber
of a Paris balcony

watching his opera beauty arrive on the arm of a strange cavalier?
To stay human is to break a limitation.
Like it if you can. Like it if you dare.

Here, Albert, this old phantom wants a proof!
Give him his proof! A camel's load of proofs!

JOHN KEATS,
Otho the Great: A Tragedy in Five Acts, 3.2.208–9

IV. HE SHE WE THEY YOU YOU YOU I HER SO PRONOUNS BEGIN THE DANCE CALLED WASHING WHOSE NAME DERIVES FROM AN ALCHEMICAL FACT THAT AFTER A SMALL STILLNESS THERE IS A SMALL STIR AFTER GREAT STILLNESS A GREAT STIR

Rotate the husband and expose a hidden side. A letter he wrote from Rio de Janeiro.

Why Rio de Janeiro? is not a question worth asking.

We had been separated three years but not yet divorced.

He turned up anywhere.

Could be counted upon to lie if asked why. Otherwise could not be counted upon.

When I say hidden

I mean funny.

A husband's tears are never hidden.

> *Rio, April 23*
> *I don't understand this business of linguistics.*
> *Make me cry.*
> *Don't make me cry.*
> *I cry. You cry. We make ourselves cry.*
>
> *Travelling foolish work spending money is what I make myself do.*
> *Carioca.*
> *I'm in an apartment in Rio with some Brazilians arguing over*
> *how to make a washing machine work.*
> *In half an hour they'll forget about it and go out for dinner*
> *leaving the machine on fire.*
> *They will come back from dinner to find their clothes burned up,*
> *slap each other on the head*

and decide they in fact bought

a dryer which they don't know how to operate.

I have just gone to look at this machine. It is indeed a washer on fire.

So now what happens. You and I.

We have this deep sadness between us and its spells so habitual I
can't

tell it from love.

You want a clean life I live a dirty one old story. Well.

Not much use to you without you am I.

I still love you.

You make me cry.

There are three things to notice about this letter.

First

its symmetry:

Make me cry. . . . You make me cry.

Second

its casuistry:

cosmological motifs, fire and water, placed right before talk of love

to ground it in associations of primordial eros and strife.

Third no return address.

I cannot answer. He wants no answer. What does he want.

Four things.

But from the fourth I flee

chaste and craftily.

one of the most mysterious of semi-speculations is, one
would suppose, that of one Mind's imagining into another

JOHN KEATS,
note on his copy of *Paradise Lost,* 1.59–94

V. HERE IS MY PROPAGANDA ONE ONE ONE ONE ONEING ON YOUR FOREHEAD LIKE DROPLETS OF LUMI-NOUS SIN

Like many a wife I boosted the husband up to Godhood and held him there.

What is strength?

Opposition of friends or family merely toughens it.

I recall my mother's first encounter with him.

Glancing

at a book I'd brought home from school with his name inscribed on the flyleaf

she said

I wouldn't trust anyone who calls himself X—and

something exposed itself in her voice,

a Babel

thrust between us at that instant which we would never

learn to construe—

taste of iron.

Prophetic. Her prophecies all came true although she didn't

mean them to.

Well it's his name I said and put the book away. That was the first night

(I was fifteen)

I raised my bedroom window creak by creak and went out to meet him

in the ravine, traipsing till dawn in the drenched things

and avowals

of the language that is "alone and first in mind." I stood stupid

before it,

watched its old golds and *lieblicher* blues abandon themselves

like peacocks stepping out of cages into an empty kitchen of God.
God

or some blessed royal personage. Napoleon. Hirohito. You know
how novelist Ōe
describes the day Hirohito went on air and spoke
as a mortal man. "The adults sat around the radio
and cried.

Children gathered in the dusty road and whispered bewilderment.
Astonished
and disappointed that their emperor had spoken in *a voice*.
Looked at one another in silence. How to believe God had
become human

on a designated summer day?" Less than a year after our marriage
my husband
began to receive calls from [a woman] late at night.
If I answered [she]
hung up. My ears grew hoarse.

How are you.
—
No.
—
Maybe. Eight. Can you.
—
The white oh yes.
—
Yes.

What is so ecstatic unknowable cutthroat glad as the walls
of the flesh
of the voice of betrayal—yet all the while lapped in talk more dull
than the tick of a clock.
A puppy

learns to listen this way. Sting in the silver.
Ōe says
many children were told and some believed that when the war was over
the emperor would wipe away their tears
with his own hand.

purple slaughter-house where Bacchus' self
Pricked his own swollen veins!

JOHN KEATS,
Otho the Great: A Tragedy in Five Acts, 5.5.123–25

VI. TO CLEAN YOUR HOOVES HERE IS A DANCE IN HONOR OF THE GRAPE WHICH THROUGHOUT HISTORY HAS BEEN A SYMBOL OF REVELRY AND JOY NOT TO SAY ANALOGY FOR THE BRIDE AS UNCUT BLOSSOM

Smell

I will never forget.

Out behind the vineyard.

Stone place maybe a shed or an icehouse no longer in use.

October, a little cold. Hay on the floor. We had gone to his grandfather's farm to help

crush

the grapes for wine.

You cannot imagine the feeling if you have never done it—

like hard bulbs of wet red satin exploding under your feet,

between your toes and up your legs arms face splashing everywhere—

It goes right through your clothes you know he said as we slogged up and down

in the vat.

When you take them off

you'll have juice all over.

His eyes moved onto me then he said Let's check.

Naked in the stone place it was true, sticky stains, skin, I lay on the hay

and he licked.

Licked it off.

Ran out and got more dregs in his hands and smeared

it on my knees neck belly licking. Plucking. Diving.

Tongue is the smell of October to me. I remember it as

swimming in a fast river for I kept moving and it was hard to move

while all around me
was moving too, that smell
of turned earth and cold plants and night coming on and
the old vat steaming slightly in the dusk out there and him,

raw juice on him.
Stamens on him
and as Kafka said in the end
my swimming was of no use to me you know I cannot swim after all.
Well it so happens more than 90% of all cultivated grapes are varieties of

Vitis vinifera
the Old World or European grape,
while native American grapes derive
from certain wild species of *Vitis* and differ in their "foxy" odor
as well as the fact that their skins slip so liquidly from the pulp.

An ideal wine grape
is one that is easily crushed.
Such things I learned from the grandfather
when we sat in the kitchen late at night cracking chestnuts.
Also that I should under no circumstances marry his grandson
whom he called *tragikos* a country word meaning either tragic or goat.

114   She] {Ha?} She   D

JOHN KEATS,
Otho the Great: A Tragedy in Five Acts, 1.3.114 *ad* 114

VII. BUT TO HONOR TRUTH WHICH IS SMOOTH DIVINE AND LIVES AMONG THE GODS WE MUST (WITH PLATO) DANCE LYING WHICH LIVES DOWN BELOW AMID THE MASS OF MEN BOTH TRAGIC AND ROUGH

All myth is an enriched pattern,

a two-faced proposition,

allowing its operator to say one thing and mean another, to lead a double life.

Hence the notion found early in ancient thought that all poets are liars.

And from the true lies of poetry

trickled out a question.

What really connects words and things?

Not much, decided my husband

and proceeded to use language

in the way that Homer says the gods do.

All human words are known to the gods but have for them entirely other meanings

alongside our meanings.

They flip the switch at will.

My husband lied about everything.

Money, meetings, mistresses,

the birthplace of his parents,

the store where he bought shirts, the spelling of his own name.

He lied when it was not necessary to lie.

He lied when it wasn't even convenient.

He lied when he knew they knew he was lying.

He lied when it broke their hearts.

My heart. Her heart. I often wonder what happened to her.

The first one.

There is something pure-edged and burning about the first infidelity in a marriage.

Taxis back and forth.

Tears.

Cracks in the wall where it gets hit.

Lights on late at night.

I cannot live without her.

Her, this word that explodes.

Lights still on in the morning.

—we imagine after it—

JOHN KEATS,
note on his copy of *Paradise Lost,* I.706–30

VIII. IT WAS JUST NIGHT LAUNDRY SNAPPING ITS VOWELS ON THE LINE WHEN MOTHER SAID WHAT'S THAT SOUND

Poets (be generous) prefer to conceal the truth beneath strata of irony

because this is the look of the truth: layered and elusive.

Was he a poet? Yes and no.

His letters, we agree, were highly poetic. They fell into my life

like pollen and stained it. I hid them from my mother

yet she always knew.

> *Lover, merciful one*
> *you write but you*
> *do not come to me.* This one my mother did not read.

> *Rabbis liken Torah to the narrow sex of the gazelle*
> *for whose husband every time*
> *is like the first time.* This one my mother did not read.

> *This is a case where he has to arouse her.*
> *This is a case where he does not have to arouse her.*
> *There is no difficulty [see illustration].* This one alas my mother read.

If it is true we are witnessing the agony of sexual reasoning in our age

then this man was one of "those original machines"

that pulls libidinal devices into a new transparence.

My mother ran counter to him as production to seduction.

When I refused to change high schools she looked at my father.

Within a year we moved to another town

and of course distance made no difference, he was at his best in letters anyway.
Secrecy an early habit, "blackmail of the deep" a molecular law.
Let's look at this.

Repression speaks about sex better than any other form of discourse
or so the modern experts maintain. How do people
get power over one another? is an algebraic question

you used to say. "Desire doubled is love and love doubled is madness."
Madness doubled is marriage
I added
when the caustic was cool, not intending to produce
a golden rule.

                                          its feet were tied
With a silken thread of my own hand's weaving

JOHN KEATS,
"I had a dove and the sweet dove died," lines 3–4

IX. BUT WHAT WORD WAS IT

Word that overnight

showed up on all the walls of my life inscribed *simpliciter* no explanation.

What is the power of the unexplained.

There he was one day (new town) in a hayfield outside my school standing

under a black umbrella

in a raw picking wind.

I never asked

how he got there a distance of maybe 300 miles.

To ask

would break some rule.

Have you ever read *The Homeric Hymn to Demeter*?

Remember how Hades rides out of the daylight

on his immortal horses swathed in pandemonium.

Takes the girl down to a cold room below

while her mother walks the world and damages every living thing.

Homer tells it

as a story of the crime against the mother.

For a daughter's crime is to accept Hades' rules

which she knows she can never explain

and so breezing in she says

to Demeter:

"Mother here is the whole story.

Slyly he placed

in my hands a pomegranate seed sweet as honey.

Then by force and against my will he made me eat.

I tell you this truth though it grieves me."

Made her eat how? I know a man

who had rules

against showing pain,

against asking why, against wanting to know when I'd see him again.

From my mother

emanated a fragrance, fear.

And from me

(I knew by her face at the table)

smell of sweet seed.

Roses in your room'd he send you those?

Yes.

What's the occasion?

No occasion.

What's going on with the color.

Color.

Ten white one red what's that mean.

Guess they ran out of white.

To abolish seduction is a mother's goal.

She will replace it with what is real: products.

Demeter's victory

over Hades

does not consist in her daughter's arrival from down below,

it's the world in bloom—

cabbages lures lambs broom sex milk money!

These kill death.

I still have that one red rose dried to powder now.

It did not mean hymen as she thought.

19   thine own   *altered in pencil possibly by Keats to*   some small

JOHN KEATS,
Otho the Great: A Tragedy in Five Acts, 1.3 *ad* 125–32

X. DANCE OF THE WESTERN UNION ENVELOPE HOW THE HEART LEAPS UP MORE EAGER THAN PLANT OR BEAST

"Devil's share" is the portion of one's goods that cannot be usefully spent

and so gets sacrificed.

But what if the devil is not so stupid.

What if a devil long after sacrifice

starts coming and going on the borderland—

just a crease in daylight.

Disappearance was a game to him,

my mother

unsurprised

when he did not appear for the wedding

and she was careful of my feelings—care

like a prong.

The wedding cake (stored in the pantry) I ate myself

piece by piece

all of it

in the months that followed, sitting

in the living room late at night with all the lights on, chewing.

His telegram (day after) said

   But please don't cry—

that's all.

Five words for a dollar.

Or June that breathes out life for butterflies?

JOHN KEATS,
"To the Ladies Who Saw Me Crown'd," line 10

XI. MAKE YOUR CUTS IN ACCORDANCE WITH THE LIVING JOINTS OF THE FORM SAID SOCRATES TO PHAEDRUS WHEN THEY WERE DISSECTING A SPEECH ABOUT LOVE

Why did nature give me over to this creature—don't call it my choice,

I *was ventured:*

by some pure gravity of existence itself,

conspiracy of being!

We were fifteen.

It was Latin class, late spring, late afternoon, the passive periphrastic,

for some reason I turned in my seat

and there he was.

You know how they say a Zen butcher makes one correct cut and the whole ox

falls apart

like a puzzle. Yes a cliché

and I do not apologize because as I say I was not to blame, I was unshielded

in the face of existence

and existence *depends on beauty.*

In the end.

Existence *will not stop*

until it gets to beauty and then there follow all the consequences that lead to the end.

Useless to interpose analysis

or make contrafactual suggestions.

Quid enim futurum fuit si. . . . What would have happened if, etc.

The Latin master's voice

went up and down on quiet waves. A passive periphrastic

may take the place of the imperfect or pluperfect subjunctive

in a contrary-to-fact condition.

Adeo parata seditio fuit

ut Othonem rapturi fuerint, ni incerta noctis timuissent.

So advanced was the conspiracy

that they would have seized upon Otho, had they not feared the hazards of the night.

Why do I have

this sentence in mind

as if it happened three hours ago not thirty years!

Unshielded still, night now.

How true they were to fear its hazards.

and evenings steep'd in honeyed indolence

JOHN KEATS,
"Ode on Indolence," line 37

XII. HERE'S OUR CLEAN BUSINESS NOW LET'S GO DOWN THE HALL TO THE BLACK ROOM WHERE I MAKE MY REAL MONEY

You want to see how things were going from the husband's point of view—

let's go round the back,

there stands the wife

gripping herself at the elbows and facing the husband.

Not tears he is saying, not tears again. But still they fall.

She is watching him.

I'm sorry he says. Do you believe me.

Watching.

I never wanted to harm you.

Watching.

This is banal. It's like Beckett. Say something!

I believe

your taxi is here she said.

He looked down at the street. She was right. It stung him,

the pathos of her keen hearing.

There she stood a person with particular traits,

a certain heart, life beating on its way in her.

He signals to the driver, five minutes.

Now her tears have stopped.

What will she do after I go? he wonders. Her evening. It closed his breath.

Her strange evening.

Well he said.

Do you know she began.

What.

If I could kill you I would then have to make another exactly like you.

Why.

To tell it to.

Perfection rested on them for a moment like calm on a lake.

Pain rested.

Beauty does not rest.

The husband touched his wife's temple

and turned

and ran

down

the

stairs.

it springs
from a man's little heart's short fever-fit

JOHN KEATS,
"Ode on Indolence," lines 33–34

XIII. IT IS A MONOPRINT BY DEGAS SHOWING A WOMAN'S HEAD FROM THE BACK CALLED *THE JET EARRING*

Inside information.
He sought her. He sought her everywhere. Through the nakednesses
of his imagination. In sorrow. In foxholes. As deer flicker way off in a wood in late
winter.

He knew he would destroy the deer.

He sought her in her virginity everywhere in it (fray'd and fled) from top to bottom
of the little looms and the whitish green and the shivering.
He sought her in the ribbon of her missal.
In the faded black smell of its sateen.
In punctuality.

He sought her in the word mistress but she wasn't there, he should
have sheltered in that doorway from the beginning but now
it was night.

He made night seek her too.

Possible night, impossible night, pegs, strings, stringing her to her own
impersonation of
him.

His hand to brush a mark from his face it was her face.

Hesitate,
oh hesitate.

In the clear panel, more he could adore,—

JOHN KEATS,
The Jealousies: A Faery Tale,
by Lucy Vaughan Lloyd of China Walk,
Lambeth, line 277

XIV. RUNNING YOUR HAND OVER IT TO CALCULATE ITS DIMENSIONS YOU THINK AT FIRST IT IS STONE THEN INK OR BLACK WATER WHERE THE HAND SINKS IN THEN A BOWL OF ELSEWHERE FROM WHICH YOU PULL OUT NO HAND

Today I have not won. But who can tell if I shall win tomorrow.

So he would say to himself going down the stairs.

Then he won.

Good thing because in the smoke of the room he had found himself wagering

his grandfather's farm (which he did not own)

and forty thousand dollars cash (which he did).

Oh to tell her at once he went slapping down the sidewalk

to the nearest phone booth, 5 a.m. rain pelting his neck.

Hello.

Her voice sounded broken into. Where were you last night.

Dread slits his breath.

Oh no

he can hear her choosing another arrow now from the little quiver

and anger goes straight up like trees in her voice holding

his heart tall.

I only feel clean he says suddenly when I wake up with you.

The seduction of force is from below.

With one finger

the king of hell is writing her initials on the glass like scalded things.
So in travail a husband's
legend glows, sings.

151   She] *written over* {He} *KRD*

JOHN KEATS,
Otho the Great: A Tragedy in Five Acts, 1.1.151 *ad* 151

XV. ANTILOGIC IS THE DANCE OF THE DOG IN HELL HAPPY TO EAT ANY FOOD THAT GROWS BUT DO THEY NOT SAY THE SAME OF A DOG IN HEAVEN

Did you tell her about me?

Yes.

And?

She wants to meet you.

Liar.

He says nothing.

Why do you come here.

He draws on his cigarette.

Parts of you (she reaches across for his pack and shakes one out) are missing.

Her name was Merced but in fact (he once told her)

You are not merciful at all.

Thin neck like birch trees, hollow of the neck.

Why do I come here. Question does not interest him.

Reddish mist is moving

in front of his eyes and a certain

raw and rowdy smell maybe oregano always in this kitchen,

always when he sits here (tingling) calm as a lamb

at the table, tingling a bit inbetween the two of them,

these two sisters, their stories, the kind of stories sisters tell.

No puede tocarle says Dolor passing behind her sister's chair.

The kind of arrangements sisters make.

What does she say? he asks Merced.

She compares you to a matador.

Out the corner of his eye he can just see the dark blue silk curve of the belly of Dolor.

Dolor the quiet one. Folds herself.

Merced is leaning forward for a light. Tell me a story Merced he says.

Hollow of the neck, hollow below the neck, its bark
almost powdery to the touch or in the dark—who can say—
these nights there were times he didn't know
if he was about to receive mercy or sorrow.

"By'r Lady! he is gone!" cries Hum "and I—
(I own it)—have made too free with his wine;
Old Crafticant will smoke me by-the-bye!"

JOHN KEATS,
The Jealousies: A Faery Tale,
by Lucy Vaughan Lloyd of China Walk,
Lambeth, lines 613–15

XVI. DETAIL AS A RETICENT EVENT

The husband had a friend named Ray whom he loved greatly.

Ray was troubled in mind but valiant.

When Ray came to the house the wife stayed in her room.

He's out of control she said.

Ray sat in the kitchen with the husband and a bottle of wine.

Talked about his "mysteries."

Tricking every night is a sign of despair

was a comment of the wife's next day at breakfast.

Ray had just left.

The husband spread his hands as if to say

Gently now.

Ray had a voice like a botched tango,

women as well as boys liked to listen to it.

And because Ray was a person

who soon enough got to know everybody

Ray soon enough got to know

Dolor and Merced.

He had some ideas about what was going on there that he kept to himself.

To the husband he said

Double your fun.

Ray liked idioms.

One night late

he came to the house looking for the husband.

The wife was in her study in the attic

with all the lights on down below.

Got your house lit up like a Roman nougat!

Ray calls out from the stairs.
She looks up from her work, deep
in the pleasure of it as he can see, something about her
blinds him.
He's out she says.
Together

they watch stray drops of this fact condense on the air between them.
Some call it love
but those two whose souls knit at that moment
as the soul of Jonathan was knit with the soul of David
did not love one another.
How much simpler that would have been.

Astounded,—*Cupid I do thee defy!*

JOHN KEATS,
The Jealousies: A Faery Tale,
by Lucy Vaughan Lloyd of China Walk,
Lambeth, line 455

XVII. SOMETIMES ABOVE THE GROSS AND PALPABLE THINGS OF THIS DIURNAL SPHERE WROTE KEATS (NOT A DOCTOR BUT HE DANCED AS AN APOTHECARY) WHO ALSO RECOMMENDED STRENGTHENING THE INTELLECT BY MAKING UP ONE'S MIND ABOUT NOTHING

Ray did not tell the wife about Dolor and Merced.

But she

had seeing scars

on her eyes from trying to look hard enough at every stone of every sidewalk in the city,

every window of every passing bus, every pane of every shop

or office block or telephone booth

to wring from it

a glimpse of the husband with someone else if such a glimpse was to be had,

if such a fact was to be faced

she wanted it over with.

Ray saw the scars and felt sad.

He thought it would not be over with for a long time yet

which proved correct.

He ticktocked the matter back and forth inside

and said very little.

You know where he's at these nights?

Sure do.

Want to tell me?

Nope.

Why's that.

You married people get too tight with things, get all strained in and sprained up.

Meaning?

Meaning don't waste your tears on this one.

This one. It's a series?

It's a gap in a series the series is you.

He says that?

Says it all the time.

And you believe it.

Was this a question? Ray thought no. He began to talk about movies.

Like to see that Brazilian film again I missed some turns.

The one about the torturers?

They call themselves generals.

Doesn't appeal to me.

It's complicated you might like it. One scene they're torturing a guy

and talking about movies at the same time movies they like

and why and one of them says You know

a good movie for me is when the enemy says something that makes sense.

Then I get scared.

Then I don't know what could happen next

and they go on torturing the guy.

How?

Dunking his head in a pail.

God Ray I don't want to see that.

Ray got up from the table and stretched. His skinny belly

showed whitish purple in the overhead kitchen light.

Got to go.

You working nights this month?

Twelve to eight Mondays off.

How's Sami?

Ray grinned his beautiful wicked grin like a skirt flying up.

Sweetness and light he said.

Sami was Ray's most recent mystery.

Sometimes Ray's mysteries

stole money and vanished breaking his heart but Sami

had not done so.

Sami rewards me said Ray.

Good said the wife.

She followed him to the door feeling a pang of abyss.

Don't be a stranger

she said and he said

'Night lady and he was gone.

Her lady shadow mounted the stairs ahead of her experimentally.

Fiction forms what streams in us.

Naturally it is suspect.

What does *not wanting to desire* mean?

Means I hope this thing is working says the wife as she sets her alarm clock

on the table by the bed.

Printing a passage in italics is a primitive way of soliciting attention

warns Fowler's *English Usage,*

appending as an example of this miserable mode of emphasis

"To Sherlock Holmes she is always *the* woman."

But emphasis is too general a word

for the dip and slant

of mindfulness

that occurs in cognition just

there: singe it.

The wife goes to the mirror.
She looks

at a wife's eyes, throat, bones of the throat.
It does not surprise her,
she cannot recall when it ever surprised her,
to realize
these bones are not bones of *the* throat.
A blush tears itself in half deep
inside her.

Otho calls me his lion,—should I blush
To be so tamed? so—

JOHN KEATS,
Otho the Great: A Tragedy in Five Acts, 4.2.42–43

XVIII. DO YOU SEE IT AS A ROOM OR A SPONGE OR A CARELESS SLEEVE WIPING OUT HALF THE BLACKBOARD BY MISTAKE OR A BURGUNDY MARK STAMPED ON THE BOTTLES OF OUR MINDS WHAT IS THE NATURE OF THE DANCE CALLED MEMORY

Rope

let down from heaven to draw me up out of not-being: Proust

used to weep over days gone by,

do you?

Gloss it.

What eyes at eagle height can see back as far as a day in March

I stood

in a doorway with him behind me his lips on my neck.

Nape of the neck.

Hole in time shows this moment to me and to you,

ragged where edges of synaptic change

melt off into

blurred walls of other days—a "flashbulb memory" neurologists say.

It has both explicit and implicit circuitry.

Note these two people

who are not yet married

stand embedded in the destiny of husband and wife as firmly

as any two contiguous molecules in a chain reaction

and he is whispering

into the place on her neck that he shaved with his own razor an hour ago—

It is very hard to be erotic with you.

Blame and shame are the name of the game

as Ray would have said, did I mention

Ray's fondness for rhyme?

But Ray wasn't there.

It was just the two of them lost together on the spiralling pathway of a husband's
beauty.

And at that moment

she began to be his downfall, if memory serves,

since he was already calm.

Better to be his downfall than not to be she thinks.

It snows that night.

She paints a red circle on each nipple

and they go out to dance in long dark rooms

for what is more true

than a snowy night, down it comes

sifting over branches and railings and the secret air itself,

down the steep, down the stops, down the deepenings, down the grooves in the nails.

They fall asleep and dream

of muffled corridors,

greenish glow

along the edges of mirrors, faces, cities.

Snow spins over it, down over it all.

he doth this moment wish himself asleep
Among his fallen captains on yon plain

JOHN KEATS,
Otho the Great: A Tragedy in Five Acts, 1.2.91–92

XIX. A CONVERSATION BETWEEN EQUALS THAN WHICH NOTHING IS MORE DIFFICULT TO ACHIEVE IN THIS WORLD HABEAS CORPUS'D AS (KEATS SAYS) WE ARE OUT OF ALL WONDER CURIOSITY AND FEAR

Coward.

I know.

Betrayer.

Yes.

Opportunist.

I can see why you would think that.

Slave.

Go on.

Faithless lecherous child.

Okay.

Liar.

What can I say.

Liar.

But.

Liar.

But please.

Destroyer liar sadist fake.

Please.

Please what.

Save me.

Who else do you say that to.

No one.

No one he says.

Have courage.

You fool.

Oh my love.

Stop.

Listen I only wanted one thing to be worthy of you.

Are you mad.

No yes it doesn't matter.

You live a counterfeit life.

Yes yes but for you.

Me.

These are my trophies my campaigns my honors I lay them before you.

The women.

Yes.

The lying.

Yes.

The shame.

No there is no shame.

The shame I feel.

There is no shame except in retreat.

Ah.

And I never retreat.

I guess not.

Be my ally.

What are we talking about now.

If you wish not to go on with this I'll stop.

Don't stop.

I've said everything before.

What's wrong with us.

Fog of war.

Why are we at war.

Because I don't want to give up.

Your dreams are a mess.

They are my masterpiece.

84

God help us then.

God has no place in war and the folly of it well one has only to persevere in folly and the world will soon enough call it success.

No it's not going to clear up is it or make sense or come out into the open somewhere this welter of disorder and pain is our life.

Yes.

Your so-called freedom.

Our so-called love.

nor our fancies in their strength can go
further than this Pandemonium

JOHN KEATS,
note on his copy of *Paradise Lost*, 1.706–30

XX. SO THE HALL DOOR SHUTS AGAIN AND ALL THE NOISE IS GONE

In the effort to find one's way among the contents of memory (Aristotle emphasizes)

a principle of association is helpful—

"passing rapidly from one step to the next.

For instance from milk to white,

from white to air,

from air to damp,

after which one recollects autumn supposing one is trying to recollect that season."

Or supposing,

fair reader,

you are trying to recollect not autumn but freedom,

a principle of freedom

that existed between two people, small and savage

as principles go—but what are the rules for this?

As he says,

folly may come into fashion.

Pass then rapidly

from one step to the next,

for instance from nipple to hard,

from hard to hotel room,

from hotel room

to a phrase found in a letter he wrote in a taxi one day he passed

his wife

walking

on the other side of the street and she did not see him, she was—

so ingenious are the arrangements of the state of flux we call

our moral history are they not almost as neat as mathematical

propositions except written on water—

on her way to the courthouse

to file papers for divorce, a phrase like

how you tasted between your legs.

After which by means of this wholly divine faculty, the "memory of words and things,"

one recollects

freedom.

Is it I? cries the soul rushing up.

Little soul, poor vague animal:

beware this invention "always useful for learning and life"

as Aristotle says, Aristotle who

had no husband,

rarely mentions beauty

and was likely to pass rapidly from wrist to slave when trying to recollect wife.

my pulse grew less and less

JOHN KEATS,
"Ode on Indolence," line 17

XXI. DO YOU EVER DREAM POOR COURT-BANKRUPT OUTWITTED AND LOST OF TERRIBLE LITTLE HOLES ALL OVER EVERYTHING WHAT DO THOSE DREAMS MEAN?

Little holes that show where the rain hits.

He was not wrong that sad anthropologist who told us the primary function of writing is to enslave human beings. Intellectual and aesthetic uses came later.

Little holes that widen and break.

Letters arrived.

Rapidly now holes multiply themselves and pour toward collision, concentrically.

By letters the husband bound her to him.

Or slow and simplify, four three two.

Letters, a natural and necessary food, arrived far less often than food should.

One.

Letters made one day different from another, made if into sun.

At the edge of the roof occurs annihilation of holes.

You know Nahum Tate rewrote *King Lear* in 1681 and his improvements took the form (besides a happy ending) of reducing occurrences of the word *if* from 247 to 33.

Along the eaves are holes striving to purchase a drop of shiny sky.

> To say what letters contain is impossible. Did you ever touch your tongue to a metal surface in winter—how it felt to not get a letter is easier to say.

Wind picks up and holes blow sideways, holoids now.

> In a letter both reader and writer discover an ideal image of themselves, short blinding passages are all it takes.

Waiting coils inside her and licks and licks its paws.

> *I go through motions already made in another life* [wrote the husband].
> *The room is cold. I must unpack. But not yet. Night is almost here.*
> *Another one without you I was going to say but that would be weak.*
> *Another one.*
> *I stand firmly on the foundation of the love I fashioned, yes our love.*
> *You will disagree. But look inside yourself. There you see a world*
> *travelling silently through space. On it two specks. We are*
> *indissoluble. Three minutes of reality! all I ever asked.*

She stands looking out at rain on the roof.

How came ye muffled in so hush a masque?

JOHN KEATS,
"Ode on Indolence," line 12

XXII. HOMO LUDENS

Omens are for example hearing someone say victory as they pass you in the street

or to be staring

at the little sulfur lamps in the grass

all around the edge of the hotel garden

just as they come on. They come on at dusk.

What was he thinking to bring her here?

Athens. Hotel Eremia.

He knew very well. Détente and reconciliation, let's start again,

thinking oysters and glacé fruits, it needs a light touch,

narrow keys

not very deep.

Hotel gardens at dusk are a place where the laws governing matter

get pulled inside out,

like the black keys and the white keys on Mozart's piano.

It cheered him to remember Mozart

borrowing money every night

and smiling his tilted smile.

Necessity is not real! after all.

The husband swallows his ouzo and waits for its slow hot snow inside him.

Mozart

(so his wife told him at lunch)

scored his Horn Concerto

in four different colors of ink: a man at play.

A husband whose wife knows just enough history to keep him going.

Cheer is rampant in the husband now.

Infinite evening ahead.

Its shoals appear to him and he navigates them one by one

slipping the dark blue keel ropes this way and that

on a bosom of inconceivable silver—ah here she is.

The husband can be seen to rise as his wife crosses the garden.

Why so sad.

No I'm not sad.

Why in your eyes—

What are you drinking.

Ouzo.

Can you get me a tea.

Of course.

He goes out.

She waits.

Waiting, thoughts come, go. Flow. This flowing.

Why sadness? This flowing the world to its end. Why in your eyes—

It is a line of verse. Where has it stepped from. She searches herself, waiting.

Waiting is searching.

And the odd thing is, waiting, searching, the wife suddenly knows

a fact about her husband.

This fact for which she had not searched

jerks itself into the light

like a child from a closet.

She knows why he is taking so long at the bar.

Over and over in later years when she told this story she marvelled

at her husband's ability to place the world within brackets.

A bracket's worth of mirage! all he ever needed.

A man who after three years of separation would take his wife to Athens —
for adoration, for peace,
then telephone New York every night from the bar
and speak to a woman
who thought he was over on 4th Street
working late.
And upstairs that night, which proved a long night, as he was dragging
his wounded honor about the hotel room like a damaged queen of moths
because she mentioned Houyhnhnms and he objected
to being "written off as an object of satire," they moved
several times through a cycle of remarks like —

What is this, what future is there
I thought
You said
We never
When exactly day year name anything who I was who I am who did you
Did you or did you not
Do you or do you not
This excuse that excuse pleasure pain truth
What truth is that
All those kilometers
Faith
Letters
You're right
Never oh all right once —

which, like the chain of Parmenides' well-rounded Truth you can follow
around in a circle and always end up where you began, for

"it is all one to me where I start—I arrive there again soon enough"

as Parmenides says. So the wife
was thinking (about Parmenides)
with part of her mind while throwing Ever Never Liar at her husband
and he was holding Yes and No together with one hand
while parrying the words of his wife when—

they stopped. Silence came. They stood aligned,
he at the door with his back to it
she at the bed with her back to it,
in that posture which experts of conflict resolution tell us ensures impasse,
and they looked at one another
and there was nothing more to say.

Kissing her, I love you, joys and leaves of earlier times flowed through the husband
and disappeared.

Presence and absence twisted out of sight of one another inside the wife.

They stood.
Sounds reach them, a truck, a snore, poor shrubs ticking on a tin wall.

His nose begins to bleed.

Then blood runs down over his upper lip, lower lip, chin.
To his throat.
Appears on the whiteness of his shirt.

Dyes a mother-of-pearl button for good.

Blacker than a mulberry.

Don't think his heart had burst. He was no Tristan

(though he would love to point out that in the common version

Tristan is not false, it is the sail that kills)

yet neither of them had a handkerchief

and that is how she ends up staining her robe with his blood,

his head in her lap and his virtue coursing through her

as if they were one flesh.

Husband and wife may erase a boundary.

Creating a white page.

But now the blood seems to be the only thing in the room.

If only one's whole life could consist in certain moments.

There is no possibility of coming back from such a moment

to simple hatred,

black ink.

If a husband throws the dice of his beauty one last time, who is to blame?

Rich proposition, drastic economy, hours, beds, pronouns, no one.

No one is to blame.

Change the question.

We are mortal, balanced on a day, now and then

it makes sense to say Save what you can.

Wasn't it you who told me civilization is impossible in the absence of a spirit of play.

Anyway what would you have done—
torn the phone off the wall? smothered him with a pillow?
emptied his wallet and run?
But you overlook
an important cultural function of games.
To test the will of the gods.
Huizinga reminds us that war itself is a form of divination.

Husband and wife did not therefore engage in murder
but continued their tour of the Peloponnese,
spending eight more wary days
in temples and buses and vine-covered tavernas,
eight days which had the internal texture of πετραδάκι (ancient πέτρος)
—that is "broken crushed stone, roadstone, gravel"—
but which served a purpose within the mode of justice that was their marriage.
Waiting for the future and for the gods,

husband and wife rested,

as players may rest against the rules of the game,
if it is a game, if they know the rules,
and it was and they did.

a sort of delphic Abstraction a beautiful thing made more
beautiful by being reflected and put in a Mist

JOHN KEATS,
note on his copy of *Paradise Lost*, 1.321

[there is a faint mark after *beautiful* read by one editor as a dash,
by another as a slip of the pen, while a third does not print it]

XXIII. HOW RICH A POOR PLEASURE TO A POOR MAN

What can save these marks from themselves.

What if we drop a little more solvent

on the seam

between foreground and background.

Ray was no Mont Sainte-Victoire

but his curiously crystalline little body

did set up a wise and fleshy relation

between world and retina.

His world your retina.

As he says himself

No one stays innocent very long around Ray.

Ray is a painter.

He cooks (most nights) at the Sincere Diner and paints by day.

When do you sleep Ray? asks the wife.

Instead of answering Ray flips two half-fried eggs with one hand

and catches an explosion of toast (too light, shoves it back down)

then spins left

to pick a clean plate off the dishwasher stack.

Clock above the pies says five to five.

Off at five Ray? I'll walk you home.

Or do you have

a date.

Ray flicks past her at the counter

and a splash of Sincere coffee fills her cup—Ray is all yours lady!

No date no wait no fate to contemplate! he grins.

Contour of a person so different from what you can get into bits of speech.

His calf muscles for instance were huge.

Like a ballet dancer's. She thought about it walking beside him.

Or a bicycle courier's.

He rolled from step to step as if on ball bearings and she knew from experience

he could walk like that half the day without tiring,

then paint for hours,

then prowl the bars.

You're strong Ray.

He nodded.

What makes you so strong.

He thought about it.

Lust he said.

You mean like Vincent van Gogh. Lust for life.

No he said. Like a bee.

Pollen she said.

He laughed.

Pollen keeps callin old Ray.

They rolled along.

Dawn was pushing the night sky up like a venetian blind

and blue

ran straight into the world from somewhere.

So you say he's phoning you lately.

Yes.

Tells you he's a better person now.

More or less.

And what else.

And he can't live without me.

I saw him at a club the other night you know he looked alive to me.

Ray what does he want me to say.

No question is what do you want him to say.

Want him to say he can't live without me.

Well bingo.

But in a way I can believe.

Now there you go knocking on heaven.

Or feel the way I feel like a body ripped in half like an incomplete state of some metal in a chemical process like a blob of scalded copper waiting to be resurrected into gold—

Don't wait for that.

Figure of speech.

He still got his clothes at your house?

Some.

Throw them out.

Can't.

You know what are the rules for this?

No.

That's because there are no rules for this. A ship passes, there's a bit of wake and some spray then it disappears.

Shut up Ray.

He spat.

Want to come in for some mashed potatoes? Then I have to paint.

They were at Ray's house.

Mashed potatoes were his usual breakfast.

No thanks Ray. What are you working on now?

Mother's Day said Ray.

Ray was painting his mother for a long time.

Portraits
on the same canvas almost four years of them,
by now a thick painting.
I like to keep the hesitation in Ray'd say.
Can I look at it? No not today.
Okay see you Ray. Bye lady.

And they were strange to me, as may betide
With vases

JOHN KEATS,
"Ode on Indolence," lines 9–10

XXIV. AND KNEELING AT THE EDGE OF THE TRANS-PARENT SEA I SHALL SHAPE FOR MYSELF A NEW HEART FROM SALT AND MUD

A wife is in the grip of being.

Easy to say Why not give up on this?

But let's suppose your husband and a certain dark woman

like to meet at a bar in early afternoon.

Love is not conditional.

Living is very conditional.

The wife positions herself in an enclosed verandah across the street.

Watches the dark woman

reach out to touch his temple as if filtering something onto it.

Watches him

bend slightly toward the woman then back. They are both serious.

Their seriousness wracks her.

People who can be serious together, it goes deep.

They have a bottle of mineral water on the table between them

and two glasses.

No inebriants necessary!

When did he develop

this puritan new taste?

A cold ship

moves out of harbor somewhere way inside the wife

and slides off toward the flat gray horizon,

not a bird not a breath in sight.

I must confess,—and cut my throat,—today?
Tomorrow? Ho! some wine!

JOHN KEATS,
Otho the Great: A Tragedy in Five Acts, 3.1.31–32

XXV. SAD SEVERE TANGO DANCE OF LOVE AND DEATH DANCE OF NIGHT AND MEN DANCE OF THE DARK KITCHEN OF THE POVERTY OF DESIRE

Shall we sharpen our eyes and circle closer to the beauty of the husband—

carefully, for he was on fire.

Under him the floor was on fire,

the world was on fire,

truth was on fire.

Around him green fire blew straight off every tree.

He was almost never sad, a god led him on.

Nor did he doubt his fate which looked as Napoleon used to say like this:

> *I write myself between worlds.*

What he wrote depended on who he was with.

Once he met Ray

he began to write paintings.

In Ray's room they worked side by side, the husband talked.

Ray liked learning about places in the world,

for he had scarcely travelled and about books,

for he did not read.

What are the Alps like?

From the plane they look fragile like pieces of pottery. Thin silences float inbetween.

And up close.

Up close more like cheese. Parmesan.

Is it expensive.

Parmesan?

Italy.

Yes and no.

You stay with your Italian sweetie?

She got married.

To who.

Man named Ricky.

They happy?

She had to unlock him she said.

Meaning sex.

I guess.

You know what's good for that is tango.

For unlocking?

Cures the digestion too.

How do you know these things.

Remember Flor?

No.

The one before Karl.

Karl?

Karl was the one before Danny.

Oh.

And Flor was a tangoist.

That seems a long time ago to me.

Poor pure Flor.

Seems so long ago.

Flor was defenseless.

Doesn't that seem a long time ago to you Ray.

No not so long but you were married then it was all different.

It makes me tremble.

What.

To think back. I remember exactly how I thought life would be.

Everyone has dreams.

No not dreams it was a precise picture.

What went wrong.

Middlemen.

Sorry?

Take the divorce for example, not her idea to divorce me. Middlemen got to her.

She knew you were lying and sleeping around.

Ray please I never lied to her. When need arose I may have used words that lied.

Way too philosophical for me.

Philosophers say man forms himself in dialogue.

That I understand.

So did she.

Now there you're wrong.

Why do you say so.

I saw her go down.

She was far stronger than me.

She went down.

Everything I did I did for her.

Why are you yelling.

I'm going to see her this weekend.

You're insane.

I'll write first.

She divorced you three years ago why not leave her alone.

I have faith.

In what.

In us.

There is no us.

Deep pure faith.

But why.

Ray you know I wish I lived in another century.

You used to say the body is the beginning of everything.

I don't believe that anymore.

You still sleep around.
I do.
You make me sad.
The way people live here—
Yes.
Land of no miracles.
What do you hope for now.
To be reborn as a great warrior in the year 3001.
On a June evening.
What did you say.
It's a line from a tango song.
On a June evening yes.

They went on working, he at his easel
and he on the floor by the lamp
while high black banks of twilight came and stood around them close
as sentries.
The husband was making a plan of the Battle of Epipolai

which he hoped to transfer to a wall of his house using acrylic paint
and small flags.
Why Epipolai? This bloody Athenian defeat
began with one surprise night move in 413 B.C.
Blurring a line between courage and folly

the Athenians attacked uphill in the dark
against fortified Syracusan positions.
Its originality at first
brought success to the plan,
then the Syracusans grasped it

and charged and disorder flowed everywhere.
Visibility was by moonlight,
they could see outlines but not who was who.
Hoplites got churning
in a space no bigger than a stairwell

for those Athenians who were already routed and descending the cliff
met others arriving fresh to the attack
and took them for enemies—moreover,
constantly shouting the password
they revealed it to the enemy and with this word

coming at them wrongly in the dark the Athenians panicked.
Friend fell upon friend.
It was like a beautiful boiling dance where your partner
turns
and stabs you to death,

cauldron of red Sicilian moon and white Greek lips.
He hums as he works.
Rectangles for the Syracusan outbuildings,
broken lines for the brave Athenian assault,
triangles for likely places of confrontation,

black dots of varying sizes for estimated casualties along the path of the rout.
In his mind
he is composing a letter
to explain to her (again)
about the fog of war and need for endurance and splendor

they will come to in the end.
We need a new password he whispers with a smile,
as he imagines himself arriving exhausted and hoarse,
dusty from the road, riding a tank one fine evening.
June evening.

"Why, Hum, you're getting quite poetical!"

JOHN KEATS,
The Jealousies: A Faery Tale,
by Lucy Vaughan Lloyd of China Walk,
Lambeth, line 559

XXVI. PROVIDED IN A SPIRIT OF UNASHAMED DIS-CLOSURE OR AS KEATS MIGHT SAY STITCHING THEIR THROATS TO THE LEAVES SOMETHING TO MAKE TIME PASS

You see me, you see my life, see what I live on—is that all I want?

No. I want to make you see time.

How shadows cross a wall and go—

by dividing pure movement into minutes, hours, years, we raise

the psuedo-problem of an underlying "self" whose successive states

these are supposed to be. Otho or not.

There was a branch I used to watch from my back kitchen window

and gradually began to keep a record of it

almost every day

in elegiac couplets,

for example:

Foaming against its own green Cheek it cools in brief

or seems to cool each Underleaf

(this was in spring, or

here's one from early October:)

Dull whitish and deadly as that Chalkline marked on the Door

by Homer who likened Carpentry to a Stalement in War

(or an overcast morning:)

Whose Shadow in abstract Rain appears to be
lashing the Wall at some secret Velocity

(just before a thunderstorm:)

This Wind at Night carrying it all over the Sky like Quartets
or Dido surviving between Lightning Sets

(early November:)

All but bare: dangling like Bits of Bone
in an All Souls Wind just five
you see those Souls seeping up the numb
Shafts, see Souls come oaring out of the Dark alive

(late November:)

Terrible Rinse, yellow Leaves, Cradle of the Shape of Fire
through early dirty drenching Snow as Mortals in tragic Attire

(expecting spring:)

Brighter than Bite
it bangs March Light too tight

(or not:)

Against this Wall, the way Brothers tear at
one another's Heads with their Love, it fought

Well I won't bore you with the whole annal.

Point is, in total so far, 5820 elegiacs.

Which occupy 53 wirebound notebooks.

Piled on four shelves in the back kitchen.

And would take maybe a night and a day and a night to read through.

With fervor.

it was the time when wholesale houses close
Their shutters with a moody sense of wealth

JOHN KEATS,
The Jealousies: A Faery Tale,
by Lucy Vaughan Lloyd of China Walk,
Lambeth, lines 208–9

XXVII. HUSBAND: I AM

a sad man and overshadowed. In the painful process of my self-discovery I want now to go deeper. No one can help me. Only I can do this. Enter the drinkable thread of life. Not since I skinned rabbits with my grandfather in the old stained sink behind the shed have I felt my perceptions so strong. Satiny red entrails. Clear splash of blood on white porcelain. Once we found unborn young just beneath the savage heart. Ah said Nono apples in the dark. He sliced them out. I was jealous. Tenderness flooded his voice.

Last time I went to see him (few months before he died) he made me sleep in the shed. Strange to have someone else in the house he said with Nana gone. Her or nothing. I was offended at first. Gradually I saw his point. Whiteness slid on the air. From the shed I watched his windows. He got up

at odd hours of the night, did push-ups. Stared out at the pines. It would have woke me. I shall have to pay for this I thought, we think we are safe. But there is no shelter. Bits of leaf trickle by. Bed's too big he said when I asked him why he doesn't sleep. No we are not secure. Necessity wins, spike by spike. I wish I could have talked to him about life and love. Silent nights. Not even a cat creaks by.

You married the wrong one was all he ever said to me by way of erotic advice. *Which wrong one?* I never asked. To combat

the resistances of language you must keep talking my analyst tells me. But to combat the swaying silence of a winter night in Nono's kitchen under the clandestine glare of the forty-watt bulb that is looped up over the red-and-white checked oilcloth on the table by a knotted cord and seems to be always slightly (like leaves on a keen and distant mountainside) vibrating though everything else in the world is still, talk is not it.

After all I married twice. He thought it obvious. Which one.

"With horror I discovered that I belong to the strong part of the world." He said this to me I think one night talking about the war. But I don't remember, I wrote it down.

Naked. Why did I say that? I want something. All my life. Want what. Everywhere I went the thing I wanted had already been scooped out. Her naked. Her uncertain edges. I could never get my fill.

She fought me. She lost.

I am married again now. To hear myself say this. The nerves know. I tried to stop it happening. Some formula to deal with the outside universe—that was years ago. I have two grown sons by this woman my present wife, they all rise early, make very strong coffee in a big carafe and sit for hours reading the newspapers. So many versions of the same story, trading sections back and forth, life has severe changes in it, none of these appear in newspapers but just the imitation of change. *Anima!*

I thought changes were holy. I spilled them like grain. How could I know. How could I know she would lose.

So this is the strong part.

A third time came they by;—alas! wherefore?

JOHN KEATS,
"Ode on Indolence," line 41

XXVIII. SOME CALL IT LOVE READ THE NEWSPAPER CLIPPING PERFORMING TO CITE (LAST TIME) KEATS *AN AWKWARD BOW*

Ray's obituary came in the mail one day (I had lost track of him)

attached to a note

in a familiar hand.

> *It was hard at the end. Ray remembered you. So do I.*
> *I read one of your old letters to him (On the Hole in My Brain) at the funeral.*
> *If you'll be in Venice in December so will I.*

No doubt you think this a harmless document.

Why does it melt my lungs with rage.

Physicists agree

there is something mysterious about the beginning of the universe.

Its *appearance of fine-tuning* they say needs to be explained.

Looking back, it's all so neat.

How many of his letters end *Rescue me* or *Don't give up*.

For example announcing the birth of his first son

and marriage to the mother he wrote:

> *This is a tragedy.*

> *There are people following me around. Just like you said.*
> *I miss you desperately love you always am*
> *sorry for everything. It all*

> *happened so fast.*

And he signs it *Husband in Exile.*
Even to receive this letter was to be transgressed
by an iridescence of him
which I could not keep out of me like a fine plaster dust
it came in at every pore.

> *My philosophy of life is that everything is as it seems—*
> *at a distance. Tanks on the edges of forests.*
> *Tanks on the edges of forests.*

The military stuff was no accident.
He knew how to rhyme every verse
with a test of virtue.

> *The only thing that can destroy us now is your cowardice.*

Tests inlaid with flattery.

> *You're the only person I'm afraid of.*

Intricate with sexual charm.

> *If you were on a whim to come and soothe me now I would be happy.*

And at the heart of it all,
the lure that makes war an addiction for some people—
that hot bacon smell of pure contradiction.

> *I hand you my fate. But don't take pity. And don't come back.*
> *This is our one chance to amaze each other.*

So you see

I work at correcting the past—

as Ray put it (title of one of his paintings) *Me and My Desire under the Red Stars*—

what was coming through the night there like holy Aphrodite orchids,

blackish red,

or apple branches with sounds of cold water rushing by them in the dark.

{Not for the glance itse}
{Not for the fiery glance itelf perhaps}
{Nor at the glance itsef}

JOHN KEATS,
The Jealousies: A Faery Tale,
by Lucy Vaughan Lloyd of China Walk,
Lambeth, written above lines 68–69

XXIX. IMPURE AS I AM (FOODSTAINS AND SHAME AND ALL) SO TOO MY CONCLUSIONS WHICH AT THE DOOR SCENT YOU AND HESITATE

To get them out of her the wife tries making a list of words she never got to say.

How have you been.

Fancy seeing you here.

I had given up hope I grew desperate why did you take so long.

Bloodless monster! had I never

seen or known your

kindness what

might I

have been.

But words

are a strange docile wheat are they not, they bend

to the ground.

Fact is,

no one was asking. Well Ray would have asked.

So for Ray let's just finish it.

Not because, like Persephone, I needed to cool my cheek on death.

Not, with Keats, to buy time.

Not, as the tango, out of sheer wantonness.

But oh it seemed sweet.

To say Beauty is Truth and stop.

Rather than to eat it.

Rather than to want to eat it. This was my pure early thought.

I overlooked one thing.

That the beautiful when I encountered it would turn out to be

prior—inside my own heart,

already eaten.

Not out there with purposiveness, with temples, with God.

Inside. He was already me.

Condition of me.

As if Kutuzov had found himself charging across the battlefield at Borodino

toward—

not the emperor Napoleon but a certain old king Midas

whose weapons

touched half the Russian army into bitter boys of gold.

Words, wheat, conditions, gold, more than thirty years of it fizzing around in me—

there

I lay it to rest.

You smile. I think

you are going to mention again

those illuminated manuscripts from medieval times where the scribe

has made an error in copying

so the illuminator encloses the error

in a circlet of roses and flames

which a saucy little devil is trying to tug off the side of the page.

After all the heart is not a small stone

to be rolled this way and that.

The mind is not a box

to be shut fast.

And yet it is!
It is!

Well life has some risks. Love is one. Terrible risks.
Ray would have said
Fate's my bait and bait's my fate.
On a June evening.
Here's my advice,
hold.

Hold beauty.

O Isle spoilt by the Milatary

[words found by John Keats scratched on the glass
of his lodgings at Newport on the night of April 15, 1817]

HUSBAND: FINAL FIELD EXERCISE CUT OUT THE THREE RECTANGLES AND REARRANGE THEM SO THAT THE TWO COMMANDERS ARE RIDING THE TWO HORSES

Hurts to be here.

"You are the one who escaped."

To tell a story by not telling it—

dear shadow, I wrote this slowly.

Her starts!

My ends.

But it all comes round

to a blue June moon

and a sullied night as poets say.

Some tangos pretend to be about women but look at this.

Who is it you see

reflected small

in each of her tears.

Watch me fold this page now so you think it is you.

Notes

"... in our unimaginative days, Habeas Corpus'd as we are,
out of all wonder, curiosity and fear ..."

JOHN KEATS,
review of *Richard III*, in *Champion*, December 21, 1818

Reference is made to the following authors and works:

Tango II: Homer, *Iliad,* 6.496.

Tango III: Jane Austen, *Jane Eyre* (London, 1847), 146.

Tango V: Kenzaburō Ōe, "Portrait of a Post-War Generation," in *Teach Us to Outgrow Our Madness* (New York, 1977); Johann Sebastian Bach, Cantata, *BWV,* 56; Rev. 7.15–17.

Tango VIII: *Babylonian Talmud Eruvin,* 54b; Jean Baudrillard, *Forget Foucault* (New York, 1987), 34; Stobaeus, *Florilegium,* 420.65.

Tango IX: "The Homeric Hymn to Demeter," in *The Homeric Hymns,* ed. T. W. Allen and E. E. Sikes (London, 1904).

Tango X: Georges Bataille, *La Part maudite* (Paris, 1967).

Tango XI: Plato, *Phaedrus,* 264; W. G. Hale and C. D. Buck, eds., *A Latin Grammar* (University of Alabama, 1903), 581a.

Tango XIII: John Keats, "The Eve of St. Agnes."

Tango XVII: John Keats, "The Poet"; John Keats, letter to George and Tom Keats, December 30, 1817, in F. Page, *Letters of John Keats* (New York, 1954).

Tango XVIII: John Keats, letter to Benjamin Bailey, March 13, 1819, in *Letters of John Keats,* ed. Robert Gittings (Oxford, 1970).

Tango XX: John Keats, "The Eve of St. Agnes"; Aristotle, *De memoria et reminiscentia,* 452a8–16.

Tango XXI: Claude Lévi-Strauss, *Tristes tropiques* (Paris, 1955), 393.

Tango XXII: Johan Huizinga, *Homo Ludens* (Lund, 1950); Nelly Sachs, letter to Paul Celan, March 10, 1958, in *Paul Celan, Nelly Sachs: Correspondence,* trans. C. Clark (Riverdale-on-Hudson, 1995); Parmenides, fr. 5 (Diels-Kranz).

Tango XXV: Thucydides, *History of the Peloponnesian War,* 7.42–59.

Tango XXVI: Samuel Beckett, *Endgame* (London, 1958).

Tango XXVII: *Anima* is a technical numismatic term used to designate the base kernel of a counterfeit coin. See Leslie Kurke, *Coins, Bodies, Games and Gold* (Princeton, 1999), 54n.27.

Tango XXVIII: John Keats, letter to Charles Brown, November 30, 1820, in *Letters of John Keats,* ed. Robert Gittings (Oxford, 1970).

A NOTE ON THE TYPE

This book was set in Meta Plus FF.

Composed by Creative Graphics,
Allentown, Pennsylvania
Printed and bound by Quebecor Printing,
Fairfield, Pennsylvania